THE NATURE KIDS GUIDE TO
GROUNDHOGS

DAVID ANDERSON

LP Media Inc. Publishing
Text copyright © 2026 by LP Media Inc.

For information address LP Media Inc. Publishing,
30012 Variolite St NW, Princeton MN 55371
www.lpmedia.org

Publication Data

Groundhogs
The Nature Kid's Guide to Groundhogs — First edition.

Summary: "Learn all about Groundhogs, the Nature Kid Way"
— Provided by publisher.

ISBN: 979-8-89818-127-7

[1. Groundhogs – Non-Fiction] I. Title.

Title: The Nature Kid's Guide to Groundhogs

CONTENTS

GRASSY GROUNDS

Squeak! A groundhog pops up from its grassy home. It looks for danger.

Groundhogs live in open areas. They like meadows and fields. They like pastures too. They also live near forest edges. These places have loose soil. Loose soil is good for digging.

Groundhogs need grass and plants nearby. They eat plants that grow near their homes. Open spaces help them see danger.

Groundhogs are also called woodchucks. The name comes from the Native American word "wuchak". It is not about chucking wood!

HOME RANGE
FUN FACT!
When groundhogs hibernate their heart rate drops from 80 to just 5 beats per minute!
6

Rustle! A groundhog munches clover in a sunny field.

Long ago, groundhogs lived mostly in forests of the eastern United States and Canada. They were not very common. They needed open spaces to find food.

Then settlers came and cut down trees. They made farms and fields. This created the perfect home for groundhogs! Now there are many more groundhogs than before.

Groundhogs keep spreading west. They now live in states like Kansas and as far north as Alaska. But they do not live in deserts. They need plants to eat and soft dirt to dig.

CHUNKY CHAPS

Thump! A chunky groundhog waddles across the lawn.

Groundhogs are medium-sized **rodents**. Adults weigh 5 to 14 pounds and grow 16 to 27 inches long. Their bushy tail adds 4 to 9 more inches!

Groundhogs are bigger than squirrels but smaller than beavers. Their bodies look round and heavy.

These animals gain weight in summer and fall. They eat a lot to get fat. The extra fat helps them survive winter sleep.

A groundhog can eat over one pound of food in a single day, about 10% of their body weight!

BUILT TO BURROW

Scratch! A groundhog digs deep with its strong paws.

Groundhogs have bodies made for digging. Their front paws have five claws. These curved claws work like shovels.

Their back legs are strong and sturdy. This helps them push dirt out of tunnels. A groundhog can move about 700 pounds of dirt to make one burrow!

Groundhogs have small ears that can close tightly. This keeps dirt out while digging. Their eyes sit high on their heads, so they can peek out of holes while staying hidden.

SHARP SENSES

Snort! A groundhog lifts its nose high. It sniffs the air.

Groundhogs have sharp senses. Their noses can smell predators from upt o half a mile away. They sniff the air often to stay safe.

Their eyes are on the sides of their heads. This gives them a wide field of view to spot danger.

Groundhogs also hear very well. They can hear high-pitched sounds that humans cannot. They even feel vibrations in the ground from footsteps above.

A groundhog can see things moving from up to 300 yards away!

TOUGH TEETH

Crunch! A groundhog gnaws on a tough root. Its strong teeth slice through.

Groundhogs have strong front teeth called **incisors**. These teeth never stop growing!

The teeth grow about one-sixteenth of an inch each week. Chewing on hard things keeps them short. Roots, bark, and stems all wear the teeth down.

These teeth are also very sharp. The front edge is harder than the back. This makes a blade-like shape for cutting plants.

Groundhogs have amazing teeth! A special coating makes them extra strong and hard.

GREENS GALORE

Chomp! A groundhog nibbles on fresh clover leaves.

Groundhogs eat mostly plants. They love green, leafy foods. Clover, dandelions, and grass are favorites.

They also eat vegetables from gardens. Lettuce, beans, and peas taste good to them. This is why farmers sometimes call groundhogs pests!

Groundhogs eat a lot in summer and fall. They can eat over one pound of food each day! All this eating helps them get fat before winter sleep.

Groundhogs sometimes even eat insects and snails when bulking up for winter!

WHISTLE WARNING

A groundhog's warning whistle can be heard up to 500 yards away – that's five football fields!

Screech! A groundhog calls out a loud warning. Others run!

Groundhogs make sounds to talk to each other. Their loudest call is a high-pitched whistle. This is why some people call them whistle pigs!

The whistle warns other groundhogs of danger. When one groundhog sees a hawk or fox, it whistles. Nearby groundhogs may stand up to look or run to their **burrows**.

But groundhogs also make other sounds. They chatter their teeth when scared. They squeal during fights. Low grunts mean they are calm and happy.

WATCH OUT!

Danger! A red fox sneaks toward a groundhog hole. The hunt is on!

Many animals hunt groundhogs. Foxes, coyotes, and bobcats chase them on land. These fast **predators** can catch groundhogs in the open.

Hawks and eagles hunt from the sky. They swoop down with sharp talons. Great horned owls hunt them at dawn and dusk.

Snakes are dangerous too. They may enter burrows to catch young groundhogs.

Groundhogs must always stay alert for danger.

A red-tailed hawk can spot a groundhog from over 100 feet in the air!

DASH AND DUCK

Zip! A groundhog runs out of its burrow. Safe at last!

Groundhogs have many ways to stay safe. Their burrows have many exits. If a predator goes in one hole, they run out another!

Speed helps too. Groundhogs can run 8 miles per hour. That is fast for chunky animals.

They also climb trees to get away from danger. Their sharp claws help them grip the bark. Groundhogs can climb 15 feet or higher! Sometimes they climb just to eat fruit or leaves They can even swim if they need to!

DIG DEEP

Rumble! Dirt flies as a groundhog digs a new tunnel.

Groundhogs are amazing diggers. They use their strong front legs to move soil. Their curved claws also help, working like shovels.

They dig long tunnels underground. Some burrows stretch over 60 feet long and go down 5 feet or more!

Digging keeps groundhogs safe. It also gives them a cool place to rest in summer.

A groundhog can move 700 pounds of dirt when digging. That's heavier than a refrigerator!

SUNNY SCHEDULES

Chirp! A groundhog comes out at dawn. Time to start the day!

Groundhogs are active during the day. They wake up at sunrise and look for food. Most of this feeding happens in the early morning.

By midday, it gets hot. So groundhogs often rest in their cool burrows. There, they may nap for a few hours.

In the late afternoon, they come out again. They eat more before sunset. Then they return underground for the night.

Groundhogs spend about 80 percent of their time in their burrows. They only come out to eat and bask in the sun!

HOG HANGOUTS

Grunt! Two groundhogs touch noses. They stand near a burrow door.

Groundhogs like to live alone. Each one has its own burrow. Each one has its own space.

But they are not always alone. A mother stays with her babies. She cares for them for weeks. Young groundhogs may share a burrow. They stay together until they grow up.

Some adult groundhogs live close by. Their burrows may be just 50 feet apart!

Groundhogs touch noses to say hello. This helps them know their family.

MATING SEASON

Snap! A male groundhog visits a female's burrow. It is early spring.

Groundhogs mate in late winter or early spring. This is soon after they wake from hibernation. Males travel to find females.

A male may visit many burrows. He goes into a female's tunnel. He often stays the night. Then he moves on to find another mate.

Mating season is short. It lasts only two to three weeks each year. After mating, females make nests in their burrows.

Baby groundhogs are born about 32 days after mating. A litter has four to six pups.

CUTE KITS

Groundhog kits leave their mother by late summer. Most are on their own by three months old!

Whoosh! The spring wind blows as groundhog kits explore.

Baby groundhogs are called kits or pups. They are born in April or May. A mother usually has 4 to 6 kits at once.

Newborn kits are tiny. They weigh only about one ounce each! They are born blind and hairless. Their eyes stay closed for about four weeks.

Kits grow fast. By four weeks old, they can see and have soft fur. Then they start eating plants and exploring outside the burrow.

MAMA MATTERS

Squawk! A mother groundhog calls her kits back inside.

Mother groundhogs work hard. They raise their babies alone, without any help from fathers.

Moms nurse their babies for about 44 days. At first, the kits drink only milk. Then they slowly start eating plants too.

Mothers teach their young important skills. Kits learn which plants are safe to eat. They also learn to watch for danger. By late summer, young groundhogs leave to find their own homes.

Groundhogs can lose up to half their body weight during hibernation!

SNOOZE TO SURVIVE

Groundhogs build a special chamber. They make a grass bed inside. They plug the entrance with dirt. This keeps them warm!

Whoosh! Cold air blows outside. A groundhog sleeps deep underground.

Groundhogs **hibernate** through winter. They curl into tight balls. They sleep in special chambers. This helps their heartbeat slow way down.

A hibernating groundhog breathes only once every six minutes. Its body gets very cold. It drops close to freezing.

This deep sleep lasts about five months. During the entire time groundhogs do not eat or drink anything!

HOG
SPOTTING
38

Click! A camera takes a picture. A groundhog stands tall.

Want to spot a groundhog? It's easier than you might think! These chunky critters love hanging out in backyards and open fields.

Your best bet is to head out early in the morning, right around sunrise. Late afternoon works well too.

Stay quiet and still, groundhogs are skittish, and any sudden movement will send them scurrying back to their burrows.

FUN FACT!

Groundhog Day is February 2nd. People watch to see if a groundhog sees its shadow!

GLOSSARY

hibernate
A deep sleep that some animals take all winter long.

burrow
A tunnel or hole that an animal digs underground to live in.

predators
Animals that hunt and eat other animals.

rodents
Animals with strong front teeth that never stop growing, like mice and squirrels.

incisors
The sharp front teeth used for biting and cutting.